IT'S TIME YOU LEFT THE SHORE

TIMOTHÉE PATON

IT'S TIME YOU LEFT THE SHORE
by TIMOTHÉE PATON

Printed in the United States of America

ISBN 9781626978706

www.xulonpress.com

Contents

Forward ... vii
Chapter 1: It's Time You Left The Shore ... 9
Chapter 2: The King Who Ripped His Clothes. ... 13
Chapter 3: Can You Carry a Stretcher? ... 17
Chapter 4: Shammah ... 23
Chapter 5: Make Sure The Bread Goes To The Back Rows. ... 29
Chapter 6: The Man Who Killed His Oxen. ... 35
Chapter 7: He Is Waiting For You At Lo Debar. ... 41
Chapter 8: Go Down Into The Valley. ... 45
Chapter 9: Have You Seen The Beggar At The Gate? ... 51

Foreword

One day I picked up *Paris Match*, a popular French magazine, and came across an interview with movie star George Clooney, known also for his humanitarian work in Africa.

The reporter asked the actor:

- **Mr Clooney, is there anything you are afraid of in life?**
- "Nothing", he replied. "I have found myself in some very dangerous situations. In Sudan, for example, a 12 year old little boy pointed a loaded rifle to my chest.

  One of my guides snatched the weapon from him just in time! Fear will never stop me.

However, what would terrify me is to wake up at the age of 75, to look back and say to myself, 'George, what on earth have you done with your life?'"

This little book you are now holding could spare you waking up one day saying to yourself, "Why in the world did I end up wasting my life?"

The short stories of Shamma, the king of Samaria, the beggar at the gate and the others are among the ones I have shared all over the world. Short stories to inspire you to live a life you won't regret.

In dozens of cities, from Sydney to Cape Town, Sao Paulo to Moscow I have witnessed hundreds of God's people responding to the call for mission.

I have seen them leave the comfort of the beach, get into the boat and move out into the greatest adventure of all.

If you haven't joined them yet, I really hope you will.

Timothée Paton
Phnom Penh, Cambodia
February 2013

Chapter 1

It's Time You left The Shore

Picture Jesus for a moment on the shore of the Sea of Galilee. As He is preaching to the crowd He notices two empty boats. One of those boats belongs to Peter.

Peter is cleaning his nets by the shore, discouraged for not having caught any fish.

Everywhere I go, I meet Christians who are sitting on the shore, discouraged. Their boat is empty.

There are probably more of God's people on the shore than in the deep end.

The longer they stay on the shore, the more discouraged they become. Their joy is drying up. Their passion for the lost is gone.

Jesus gets into Peter's boat and after speaking to the crowd, turns to Peter and says, ***"Now, go out where it is deeper and let down your nets, to catch some fish." (Luke 5:4 NLT)***

You cannot spend all your time on cleaning your nets. You cannot stay on the beach forever. It's time to move out of the shore.

What is the name of your shore–Disappointment? Self pity? Depression? Comfort?

Jesus is already in the boat. He's calling you.

God needs you. The boat cannot leave without you.

Five meters from the shore is not enough nor is fifty meters. If you want to catch many fish, you need to head for the deep end.

What deep end is God calling you to? Reaching into prisons? Ministering to the sick and dying? Bringing God's love into schools?

Who's going to cast their nets among the 10,807,000 Patahn people of Afghanistan where only 0.01 percent are known to be followers of Jesus?

Who's going to the deep end of Chad where 1,258,000 souls from the Shuwa people group are living in complete darkness? There's over 2 million White Moors of Morocco among which there are no known believers.

Hudson Taylor once said, "I am unable to bear the sight of a congregation of a thousand or more Christians rejoicing over their own salvation while millions are perishing–lost."

We cannot stay on the shore when we know the facts.

It's time to leave the crowd and launch into the deep end.

I got an email from a Dutch couple who have gone to WEC's Missionary College in Holland. They are leaving the shore for the deep end. They wrote, "This week in class we learned about children in crisis. We want to make a difference for them. It might just be one child at a time. That alone is already worth giving up our house and possessions."

In 1999, I left France for the deep end of Cambodia. With a bunch of dedicated friends we are casting our nets in the city of Phnom Penh where thousands of children are forced every day to work on the streets for a living.

Over the years in Cambodia, there have been times when my boat was tossed by strong winds. At times some water does get into the boat. Jesus never said we would not have any storms or trials but He said He would be with us.

You won't drown. Jesus is in the boat.

"Let down your nets," says Jesus to Peter, ***"to catch some fish."***

All of us have a net–the talents and gifts the Lord has blessed us with.

Don't cast your net on the sand. You won't catch anything. Well, maybe a dead fish and a few shells.

Cast your net into the deep end. Use your talents where you'll find the fish.

In 1885, at the age of 19, John Keith Falconer went out as a missionary to the Arabians. He wrote, "I have, but one candle of life to burn, and I would rather burn it out in a land filled with darkness than in a land flooded with light."

Our nets are not to be on display. A net hanging on a wall might remind you and your friends of the good days spent at sea, but your net is of no use.

Your nets have probably been on display for a long time. Take them back to the sea. Don't waste your God-given abilities!

And as you go and serve God, there's a promise from Jesus Himself, ***"You will catch fish."***

In a refugee camp in Sudan, you will catch fish. On a rubbish dump in Bangkok, you will catch fish. In a crowded Afghan hospital or among thousands of foreign students in a European university, you will catch fish.

The Lord will provide other workers to help you pull the nets in. Others from the body of Christ will join in to gather the catch! Other fishermen came over to Peter's boat, ***"And soon both boats were filled with fish." (Luke 5:7 NLT)***

When you decide to respond to the Call of going into all the world and preach the Gospel, you won't make everyone happy.

When you leave the crowd you might upset a few.

One day a man on holiday in the Bahamas noticed a big crowd gathered at the end of a pier. As he got closer he observed someone preparing for a solo journey around the world in a tiny boat. Everyone watching was telling him all the things that could go wrong. Suddenly the man felt a strong urge to offer some encouragement. So, as the little boat drifted away into the sea, he began jumping up and down on the pier, "Go for it! You can make it! We're proud of you!"

As you launch into the deep end you will hear The Voice telling you, "Go for it! You can make it! We're proud of you!"

Chapter 2

The King Who Ripped His Clothes

This is the kind of story you don't read to your children before they go to sleep.

Samaria. A high walled-fortified city.

One day an army comes and launches a siege.

No one in Samaria can come out. The city is surrounded with troops.

After a few days, food prices go up and it won't be long before the smell of death starts creeping into every home. Only the rich can now afford to buy what is left on the market stalls.

There's a king in Samaria. He feels terribly helpless. He might be king but he can't help his people.

The Bible tells us that, ***"One day the king of Israel was walking along the city wall. A woman cried out, 'Help! Your majesty!'***

He answered; 'If God won't help you, where on earth can I go for help?'

The king continued, 'Tell me your story.'

She said: 'This woman came to me and said, 'Give up your son and we'll have him for today's supper; tomorrow we'll eat my son.' So we cooked my son and ate him. The next day I told her, 'Your turn- bring your son so we can have him for supper.' But she had hidden her son away.''' (2 Kings 6: 26-29 The Message).

The king must have heard some terrible stories lately but this one was beyond anything he had heard.

I don't think you can go any lower than that: mothers deciding to have their sons for supper!

The Bible says: ***"When the king heard this, he tore his clothes in despair." (2 Kings 6: 30 NLT)***

When you hear the horror stories on the news almost every day, how do *you* react? How do you respond to the millions of children caught in the sex slave trade or to the multitudes of souls living in slums like animals in cages? How do you respond to Christians across the Communist and the Muslim world, who, because of their faith, have ended up locked in small, filthy prisons cells?

Does it break your heart? Does it move you to the extent that you cannot help, but rip your clothes too?

A.B. Simpson, a great missionary of the past, often hugged a globe to his chest and wept over the world's lost-ness.

Everywhere I go, I meet people who are moved by the needs and touched in their hearts by the suffering in the world. But very few truly end up tearing their hearts.

If someone is to ask me, "Timothée, how do I know where God wants me to serve Him? There are great needs everywhere, where should I go?"

I will answer them, "If a group of people, a community, a city, a specific country, something literally breaks your heart, then this is very likely where God wants to use you."

Too many of God's people have only unbuttoned their shirts during a short term mission trip overseas or at a church outreach in their community. It's good, but more is needed. Your clothes have to be torn from the top to the bottom.

Thankfully in Samaria there's a man of God. He announces that the next day, the troops will have gone, the famine will be over and the gates of the city will be wide open. And it happened just as the prophet had said.

This is what I see here–the very day after the king ripped his robe, the gates of the city were ripped open too.

Friends, the day your heart is ripped open, the gates to your destiny will open up. No one will be able to stop you from running into your calling.

Some people have prayed for years asking God to open the doors but few of them are really willing to pay the price. Ripping your clothes will cost you but the blessings you'll reap will be countless.

2000 years ago, the King of kings ripped heaven open to come down into our world. On the way to the Cross His clothes were ripped. His heart was ripped.

The Temple curtain was ripped. Jesus is calling for "ripped-clothes, ripped-heart followers".

If your heart is already torn, keep it torn. Don't go looking for a needle and a thread to sew it up again. Keep your heart on fire for Jesus and for the lost. Don't let anyone try to make you look more respectable by giving you a new shirt.

The day Samaria opened up again, the crowds like a mob came pouring out through the gate. In that joyful crowd I'm sure there was that boy, the one those two mothers had planned to eat. His life was spared.

Today millions of boys and girls are trapped in the jaws of death. You'll find them in dark rooms in Karachi or Dhaka making carpets from dawn to dusk. You'll find them locked up in brothels in New Delhi. You'll find them eating out of rubbish bags in Kampala and Mexico City. But they don't have to die. There is, for each one of them, the promise of a new life.

Let your heart break today with what breaks the heart of God. And by all means keep it broken.

Chapter 3

Can You Carry A Stretcher?

People started running all over Capernaum when they heard He was in town.

Children leaving the playground. Mothers leaving their kitchen. Students running out of their classroom. They were all heading to that one house where the Healer was holding a service. Those who got there late probably could not see the Master but could hear His words of hope.

Somewhere else in town, there is another house. That one I guess is very quiet. There's only one man living there. He's crippled. There is no way he is going to get to where Jesus is. His road is quiet too, as everyone has gone to see the One they might never see again.

I can picture him saying to himself, "If only Jesus had chosen my house to hold His meeting. How can I let this unique opportunity slip away?"

A crippled man. All alone.

That's much the way our world looks today. There are crippled lives everywhere. People are dying, alone, without any hope for this life or for the next.

I live in a crippled country. After being crippled for so long by one of the worst genocides in history, Cambodia is now crippled with corruption, greed and injustice. On the streets and in the slums of Phnom Penh, I meet crippled people every day.

Around the world, there could now be up to 200 million children living on the streets. From Dakar to Dacca, multitudes of boys and girls, crippled and alone.

Four men decide to do something. They'll be late for the service, but it doesn't matter. Jesus could be gone when they get there, but they are going to try it anyway.

They get the crippled man on a stretcher and carry him down the streets.

We don't know who those four men are. Neighbors? Family members? One thing we do know, they have something in their spirits. A compassion that compels them to action.

Your title and position don't matter, the diplomas or degrees hanging on your office wall don't mean a thing, if you're not picking up a stretcher and bringing broken lives to Jesus.

When those 4 friends get to where Jesus is teaching, the house and the entrance to the house are packed with people.

When you decide to pick up a stretcher and serve God, you'll find a few 'overcrowded door entrances'.

But if you're serious about the lost, the least and the last, you'll find ways to bring them to Jesus (sometimes innovative and odd ones)!

You'll even see stairs along the wall leading to the roof.

Getting a sick man on a stretcher up a flight of stairs is not an easy job.

A number of times, when working among the poor in Cambodia, I have found myself wondering, "How in the world are we going to get this child, this family up the stairs?" How many times have I got stuck halfway up the stairs, wondering what to do next.

They finally made it to the top. The roof is closed (how could it be otherwise)?

They are so determined to get their friend to Jesus, that they break the roof open.

The only way some crippled lives are ever going to meet Jesus, the only way un-reached people groups are ever going to hear the Gospel, is when men and women, who are passionate for God, bypass protocol and break some roofs.

D.L Moody once said: *"The world has yet to see what a man totally committed to God can do."*

The reason why countries like Brazil or Argentina are seeing phenomenal church growth today is very much because, back in the 50s, small groups of believers, in spite of persecution, did just what those 4 men of Capernaum did. They broke some roofs (and rules at the same time)!

The day you gave your life to Jesus, you were given a stretcher.

Sadly too many Christians have never picked it up. Some die and go to Heaven without ever using it. God has equipped you with tools, talents and a testimony to get busy for Him.

The ***majority*** of God's people prefer sitting in 'a packed house'. They never do anything for Jesus outside of church. Another conference in their church. Another concert in their church. Another seminar in their church. Another 'Me Centered Christianity' speaker in their church.

I want to belong to *the* ***minority***. Those who have decided to spend their lives carrying a stretcher.

I once got a newsletter from an elderly couple serving with a mission to children-at-risk. They wrote, *"Can we challenge you to consider that retirement, meaning doing little or nothing is a 'man-made' concept and not found in the Scriptures. Each of us can do something wherever He has placed us in the world and under whatever circumstances, until He calls us home."*

It was in 1986 in Clermont-Ferrand, Central France. I was 13 years old, my brother 14. We discovered in a small room at the back of our church a bunch of gospel posters rolled up on a shelf, covered with dust.

"Why don't we go out and stick them up on those free advertisement boards in town?" We said to each other.

We bought some wall paper glue and got on our bicycles.

When we got all those posters up, we decided to create our own. A friend from church helped us design them. At the photocopy shop we got thousands of small posters made. All over town and beyond, people could read messages such as *"Jésus Revient Bientôt"* (Jesus is Coming Back Soon)and *"Lisez la Bible"* (Read the Bible).

Young people from the church joined in and the poster work grew.

Two years later, I noticed how many free newspapers we were getting in our letter box every week. You would find all kinds of announcements from second hand cars for sale to astrologers and mediums promising you health and wealth. I felt the Christian message should also be in there. I went to one of the newspapers in town, wrote a Bible verse on a paper and handed it over the counter. "Can I pay for this message to get into your newspaper?" I asked the lady.

To my surprise she said yes.

When I spotted the newspaper in my letterbox the following week, I rushed through the pages to look for the Bible verse. It was there!

That got me really excited. "I'm going to get another one in. And not just in that newspaper but in the other ones too!" I told myself.

From there *"L' Évangélisation Par les Affiches et les Journaux"* (Evangelism Through Posters and Newspapers) was born.

That small outreach grew so much that over the years Christians in France and all over French-speaking Africa got on board. Only Heaven will tell how many people found Christ through this simple ministry.

All my brother and I did was simply pick up a stretcher and get busy.

There are too many men and women of God carrying a stretcher all by themselves. You'll find them caring for orphans in poverty-stricken Haiti; ministering to drunkards on the streets of Manchester or London; you'll find them planting a church in a remote Romanian village or working alone translating the Scriptures among some forgotten tribes. They need you to go and help them carry the stretcher.

The day you get hold of the stretcher, you will never want to let go of it.

Chapter 4

Shammah

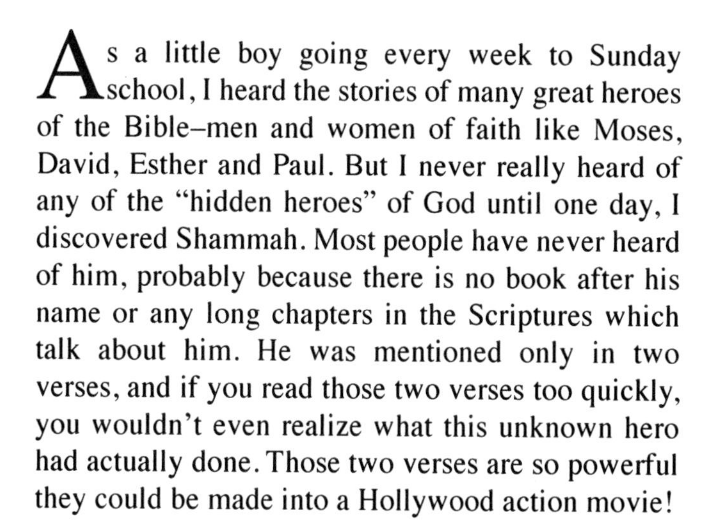

As a little boy going every week to Sunday school, I heard the stories of many great heroes of the Bible–men and women of faith like Moses, David, Esther and Paul. But I never really heard of any of the "hidden heroes" of God until one day, I discovered Shammah. Most people have never heard of him, probably because there is no book after his name or any long chapters in the Scriptures which talk about him. He was mentioned only in two verses, and if you read those two verses too quickly, you wouldn't even realize what this unknown hero had actually done. Those two verses are so powerful they could be made into a Hollywood action movie!

"Next in rank was Shammah son of Agee from Harar. One time the Philistines gathered at Lehi and attacked the Israelites in a field full of lentils. The Israelite army fled, but Shammah held his ground in the middle of the field and beat back

the Philistines. So the Lord brought about a great victory." (2 Samuel 23: 11-12 NLT).

The Israelites are about to face the Philistines on a field of lentils (interesting place for a battlefield)! For some reason, the whole army of Israel fled from the battlefield. Why did they run away? Were they out-numbered? Was the enemy better equipped?

All fled the field. All except one man, Shammah–A True Hero.

Most of us would have run with the rest of the army. Nobody in their right mind would have stayed by themselves in the middle of the battle field.

Nobody in their right mind would spend their lives translating the Bible among some lost tribe in the middle of nowhere. Nobody in their right mind would go to Albania, Europe's poorest country, learn the language and establish a church. Nobody in their right mind would spend all their time and resources to helping HIV AIDS children in an African war zone. Nobody in their right mind would spend years after years reaching out to broken families in Phnom Penh's slums like the volunteers helping day in and out at "The Bong Paoun Project".

The Church of Jesus Christ is still at war. Our enemy is real. When faced with the challenge, we can either run away with the crowd or stay back and take our stand in the middle of the field.

History is full of "unknown heroes" who like Shammah, have made a difference in God's Kingdom.

You have probably never heard of Charles Loring Brace. I never had till a couple of years ago when I came across his story.

Imagine yourself as a child, abandoned on the streets of New York City. Your immigrant parents died on a ship on the way to America or of sickness in the city. You have no money and no relatives. You can't speak English and you don't know how you'll get your next meal.

Thousands upon thousands of orphans in the 1850s found themselves caught in that kind of life. They slept in dark streets, huddling for warmth in boxes or metal drums. To survive, they mostly stole, caught rats to eat and went through garbage.

Immigrants were flooding New York City then, and no one had time or money to look after orphans; no one except Charles Loring Brace, a 26 year old minister. Horrified by their plights, he began the Foster Home Plan. When he ran out of homes, he organized a unique solution–The Orphan Train. The idea was simple: put hundreds of orphans on a train heading west. As the train passed through towns along the way, Christian committees would bring approved Christian families to the train stations to claim a son or daughter from the Orphan Train.

By the time the last Orphan Train steamed west in 1929, between 150,000 and 200,000 children had found new homes and new lives. Two orphans from those trains became governors, one served as a United States congressman, the other became a U.S Supreme Court Justice.

Charles Loring Brace took his stand in the middle of the field.

There's a field of lentils for you. If you are not in one yet, go out looking for one. It won't be long before you'll find yours.

I was listening the other day to a sermon of Evangelist Reinhard Bonnke speaking at a large conference in Singapore. He said, "*Some people at every conference get a new calling from God. You don't need another calling from God. You need to go to the shopping mall and buy yourself a suitcase and get going!*" Everyone in the audience cheered, but I wonder how many actually did "get going".

A few years ago, an average 16 year old American was spending 51 hours every week watching TV, videos, movies and on the internet (thank God I grew up without a TV)! Make every hour of your life count for what really matters. Don't waste it. Go join Shammah on the field.

For those of you who are still in the middle of the field, I want to encourage you not to leave. Don't quit. The same Holy Spirit who has called you and equipped you is still with you today. The Philistines won't win; Jesus is on your side. Whether you are trying to establish a Christian Outreach at some large university or making Him known in the world of politics, sports, media or the arts and entertainment, you are not alone.

"But Shammah held his ground in the middle of the field and beat back the Philistines".

Did you get that? Not only did he face the whole army, he beat them! It's not one man beating another man. It's one man beating a whole army!

You have no idea what God will do through ***you*** on a field of lentils!

Chapter 5

Make Sure Your Bread Goes To The Back Rows

On one hand you have thousands of hungry people–men, women and children. On the other hand, a young boy.

We don't know where this boy is from, what his name is or how old he is.

However this is what we do know–he has 5 loaves of bread and two fish, which he probably kept inside a small basket.

What he has, he gives to Jesus.

This boy's simple act of obedience is the key to a miracle.

I want to invite you to look up and see the masses of hungry faces, where you live and beyond, who until this day have still never had the opportunity to hear the Good News of the Gospel. 20% of the world's population are caught in the grip of Islam, 15% are under the shadow of Hinduism.

Look in your hands. You and I have a basket. We have gifts and talents God has blessed us with. Some of us have one fish. Some of us have a fish and a piece of bread. Others have been blessed with 4 or 5 loaves of bread.

When I was 12 years old, I discovered I had "a piece of bread and a fish in my basket":

At a scout camp, in the French Alps, I gave my first sermon, my first 'piece of bread'. I actually spoke on this story of the boy who gave the little he had to Jesus. I did not speak for very long but how great I felt!

That same year I started writing short children stories that ended up being published in various Christian magazines and printed as gospel tracts. I had found a 'fish in my basket'.

There are too many Christians today who are keeping their basket to themselves. Their fish is rotting. Their loaf of bread has gone stale. They will die with a basket full of rotten gifts.

The greatest tragedy in the Church today is having millions of Christians holding onto a basket while a huge portion of the world's population is dying from spiritual famine.

You can either be so overwhelmed with the needs that you keep your talents to yourself, or you can let Jesus take your life and use it to bring the Bread of Heaven to a lost world.

Jesus' disciple, Andrew, after seeing the small amount of food the boy had, said, ***"What good is that with this huge crowd?" (John 6:9 NLT)*** Andrew should have known better.

Do not let anyone look down on you and on the gifts God has blessed you with. Don't let anyone's 'wisdom' hinder you from going out to serve Jesus.

The city of Birmingham in England is known for Cadburys, one of the world's most famous chocolate brands.

Its founder, Richard Cadbury, had a daughter called Helen. A century ago, when Helen was 13 she went along with her father to a mission hall he had built in a poor area of the city. That Sunday evening she responded to the preacher's invitation to trust in Jesus. Immediately she wanted to share her faith with her school friends. She put her Bible on her desk 'to show what God said, rather than what I thought'.

Her friends started to turn their lives to Christ. Within two years, Helen founded the "Pocket Testament League" (PTL).

When Helen got married, she and her American husband Charles traveled the world, sharing the Gospel.

Millions of copies of the Gospel of John were distributed through PTL missionaries in Japan and Germany following World War 2. The pilot who led Japan's attack on Pearl Harbor, Mitsuo Fuchida, became a Christian after reading a PTL's Gospel of John.

Today PTL works in 25 different countries.

And it all started when a young girl gave the little she had to serve Jesus.

Just go back with me to the story of the feeding of the five thousand.

A Norwegian evangelist who ministered much in Africa till he died a few years ago, shared the following analogy:

Imagine that the story had actually been different from what we know it in the Scripture.

Jesus fills the disciple's baskets. They go and share the food with the people sitting in rows on the grass.

They start with the first row. Everyone in the first row gets their share. Then they go on to the second row and then the third. By then the baskets are empty, so the disciples go back to Jesus who fills them with more fish and more bread.

Philip, Andrew and the others go back to the people but instead of going to the fourth row, they start from the first row again. They serve row number 1, number 2 and number 3. Their baskets are once again empty.

They go back to Jesus. He fills the baskets again.

All day long, until the sun goes down, only the first three rows were being served.

What do you think the people in the back rows would have said?

"Hey! What's going on here? How is it that those in the front rows are being served again

and again while we haven't had any food yet!"

Thankfully this is not what happened. We all know the story.

The tragic fact is, this is what is happening across the Christian world today. Most churches are serving the front rows again and again and again, while over

2 billion souls are still waiting in the back rows for a single piece of bread.

87% of all mission work and finances is still going out to peoples and nations who have heard the Gospel over and over again.

God is looking for men, women and children who will make the back rows their priority.

Oswald Smith said, "Why should some hear the Gospel twice when others have never heard it even once?"

A friend of mine from Scotland has been reaching out for many years to the nomads in Northern Chad. She is the only missionary among 250,000 Muslims in that region. She sleeps in tents and travels through the desert. She is bringing Jesus to the back rows.

Don't spend the rest of your life on the front rows. Millions are hungry in Chad, in Libya, in Tajikistan, in Oman, in Turkey, in Japan. They have the right to the Bread of Life.

I invite you to pray, "*Lord, if you can use the young boy in the Gospel you can use me. I give you my bread and my fish. Take my life and use me. I respond to the Call to go to the back row, wherever that may be. I will never lack bread for You will faithfully provide as I faithfully serve you. In Your Name I go.*'

Chapter 6

The Man Who Killed His Oxen

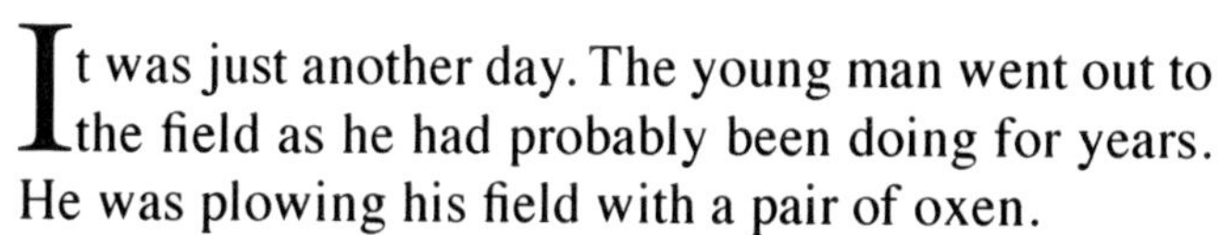

It was just another day. The young man went out to the field as he had probably been doing for years. He was plowing his field with a pair of oxen.

Elisha was a farmer and one day he would eventually take over the family business.

Elisha had no idea that on that day, his life would never be the same again.

A whole new chapter was about to unfold. A chapter that had not been planned at all. It all happened when an old man, with a similar name as the young farmer, came upon the field that day.

Elijah, an anointed prophet of God, threw his cloak over Elisha's shoulders.

That very same day, the young farmer killed his oxen and invited his friends for a farewell BBQ. He kissed his Mum and Dad goodbye and followed the old man into a whole new world.

Elisha could have stayed on his farm for the rest of his life.

Peter, Andrew, James and John could have stayed on the shore of Galilee for the rest of their lives. Instead they left their nets and followed Jesus.

David Wilkerson could have stayed in the comfort of his home. Instead he brought the Gospel to some of the worst gangs in New York.

Jackie Pullinger could have stayed her whole life in England. Instead she traveled on a ship that took her all the way to Hong Kong. 40 years later, she is still there ministering to men caught in the web of drug addiction.

The Bible says that ***'Elisha returned to his oxen and slaughtered them.' (1 Kings 19:21 NLT)***

What is the name of your oxen?

What is it that is holding you back from following Him? A relationship? A comfortable life? An addiction? Bitterness?

If you don't put your oxen on the altar as a sacrifice you can never fully serve God. Don't even hide the oxen in a small barn somewhere, because when the ride gets rough, you will run back to it.

Don't worry how God will provide for you. He *will* provide! Since I've been in Cambodia I've had no salary. But I've never lacked. God has been faithful.

The old prophet has now taken Elisha as his young disciple.

In 2 Kings Chapter 2 you find them traveling together.

At a place called Gilgal, the old mentor tells the young man, ***"Stay here, for the Lord has told me***

to go to Bethel." Elisha turns around and says, ***"As surely as the Lord lives and you yourself live, I will never leave you!" (2 Kings 2:2 NLT)***

They both then head off for Bethel where the very same scenario happens again. Elisha will not stay in Bethel; he will follow his teacher to Jericho.

In Jericho, the same thing.

Elisha is not settling in Jericho. He is heading for the Jordan because that's where God's anointing is.

Burning your oxen and saying goodbye to your farm is good.

But as you walk with the Great mentor Jesus, you can end up stuck in Gilgal. You feel the Lord is blessing you, you have brought some souls to Christ, you attend a good church but after some time you reach a plateau.

Some Christians have been stuck in the 'Gilgal Christian life' for years.

Don't stop halfway. Don't die in Gilgal or in Jericho. Head for the Jordan!

I have met many believers, even missionaries who, though they had left the comfort of their farm, got stuck somewhere between Gilgal and the Jordan.

They never made it to the River!

During the reign of Oliver Cromwell the English Government ran low on the silver it needed to make coins. So Cromwell sent his men into the cathedrals to search for some. They reported back that the only silver they could find was in the statues of the saints standing in the corners. Cromwell sent back word, "Good, let's melt down the saints and put them into circulation."

We are called to be melted by God, filled with His Spirit and put into circulation into a world that desperately needs Jesus.

Between each town on his way to the Jordan, Elisha was faced with groups of prophets. They became a pain in the neck by reminding him that his mentor would soon be taken away from him.

As you move into your next level of service with God, you'll meet the so called prophets who will try to slow you down.

They will tell you, "You're too old now to serve the poor in India."

They'll tell you, "Your CV is not good enough to start a church in Paris."

They'll tell you, "Forget about ministering to prisoners. Your own past is worse than some of those inmates."

Don't let anyone, whatever title or position they may have, distract you from going all the way with God. Don't compromise your vision! Don't settle for average.

Our world is in great need of the Gospel. Go where the need is the greatest.

I remember meeting a young man in New Zealand some years ago. He said, "I will soon be going out to the mission field, but not to a place already reached with the Gospel. I have gone through a whole list of countries to look for those with less than 1% believers and I will go to one of those places." (Dear Kiwi friend, if you're out there and you're reading this, I hope you've made it to that place of service !)

One day, I was speaking at an International Christian School in Phnom Penh (a few minutes' drive from where I live). At the end of the message I gave a call for the students to dedicate their lives for God's service. Among those who responded was a young Korean lad, "In a few years' time," he told me, "I will be a missionary to Saudi Arabia."

Where are you today? Still on the farm? In Gilgal? Sitting on the roadside?

I encourage you to move out, in faith. Go for it! He is with you!

Chapter 7

He Is Waiting For You At Lo Debar

David is king. From his palace in Jerusalem he remembers Jonathan. They were best friends back in their youth. Jonathan is dead but the love between David and Jonathan has not died. David calls one of his servants, Ziba, who was working for the previous king, Saul, father of Jonathan and asks, ***"Is anyone still alive from Saul's family? If so, I want to show God's kindness to them."***

Ziba replies: ***"Yes, one of Jonathan's sons is still alive, but he is crippled in both feet."***

"Where is he? " (2 Samuel 9:3-4a)

The Bible goes on to say that when King David heard that Mephiboseth was living in a place called Lo Debar, he calls Ziba to head off for Lo Debar, find Mephiboseth and tell him to come and live at the palace.

Mephiboseth:

Across the world today, there are millions of lives like Mephiboseth–broken, bruised, sick and lost. Mephiboseth is the prisoner, like the ones I meet in broken down Cambodian prisons. Mephiboseth is the young girl who sells her body on the streets for a few dollars. Mephiboseth is that baby who's been diagnosed with an incurable disease. Mephiboseth is that unreached people group who are living far from God: the Afghani Tadjik people (4 million of them) or the Shawiy of Algeria (1.6 million of them).

Mephiboseth does not know that Jesus Himself is calling him to His kingdom. There's a seat at the Father's table for each Mephiboseth of the world.

Lo Debar:

Most Christians are too busy to find out where Lo Debar is. Some might pray for the unreached people of the earth but very few will ever go there. The name 'Lo Debar' actually means 'No pasture'.

Lo Debar is that slum in the Philippines where people, like beasts, are stacked on top of each other. Lo Debar is that remote village in Turkmenistan where, to this day no one has yet made Christ known. Lo Debar is that town in Italy where unemployment, drugs and crime are holding many in bondage.

It is always easier to stay in the comfort of the palace than to head out for Lo Debar.

Ziba:

Ziba, David's servant did not look for someone to replace him on his mission. He did not look for any excuse. He promptly responded to the call, the way Isaiah the prophet responded, *"I'll go! Send me." (Isaiah 6:8 The Message)*

Back in the 60s my mother left her home in England and crossed the Channel. A couple of years later my father moved out from Scotland and also headed for France. Both responded to God's call to mission. They have dedicated their lives and resources to sharing the Gospel of Christ and planting churches among the French people. It has often been tough, it has been rough but they have never looked back. For almost 50 years France has been their Lo Debar. They are still there today.

Have you found ***your*** Lo Debar?

Many Christians think that Mephiboseth is going to arrive all by himself just like that, at the doorstep of the palace. Jesus never said the lost will come by themselves. He said. ***"Go into all the world and preach the Good News to everyone!" (Mark 16:15 NLT)***

Do you remember the Ziba God sent to you? The Ziba who led you to Jesus? Was it a friend from work? A neighbor? A missionary? Do you still remember the day when you walked through the doors of the palace, and in spite of your broken life, Jesus welcomed you to His table?

There is a long table in God's palace: Around the table are men, women and children of all races, from every language. They are sitting in the palace because one day, someone found them in Lo Debar. They are no more orphans. Today like you and me, they belong to God's great family.

But around God's table, there are still many empty seats. We cannot yet celebrate because those afar have still not responded to God's invitation.

Hudson Taylor, one of the first missionaries to China, tells the story of how a young Chinese Christian, who had recently become a follower of Jesus, came up to him one day and asked, *''Mr. Taylor, since how long is the Good News of the Gospel known in your country?"*

"In England where I came from," answered the missionary, *"we've known about Jesus since a long, long time ago. Actually hundreds of years."*

"Hundreds of years!" exclaimed the young Chinese, astonished. *"And no one from your country ever came to tell us about Jesus!"* And he added with much sadness in his voice, *"My dad searched for the truth his whole life. He searched and searched but he died without finding it. Oh! Why did you not come to China sooner?"*

God bless you as you reach out for Him, in Lo Debar.

Chapter 8

Go Down Into The Valley

On one hill is the army of the Philistines.
On another hill the army of Israel.
Thousands of soldiers facing each other.

Between those two armies, a valley.
The valley will soon become a battlefield.

In the ranks of the Philistines there is a warrior and a champion. A giant of a man.

Every morning and every evening Goliath comes down alone onto the battlefield. He looks up to the Israelites and shouts, ***"I defy the armies of Israel today. Send me a man who will fight me!" (1 Samuel 17:10 NLT)***

When he finishes his speech, he heads back to his camp. Goliath goes through that same scenario every day, for 40 days.

When King Saul and all of the Israelites hear the words of the Philistine, they are terrified.

They are God's people. God's army. Anointed for battle. But when one man comes down into the valley they are paralyzed with fear!

In God's Church today there are a lot of people on top of the hill. Most of them are enjoying great worship. Attending great conferences. Reading good Christian books.

They are well equipped and anointed for battle. But when the giants come onto the battlefield, they freeze.

There are so many valleys in our world today, where giants of all kinds are still defying the Name of God:

The valley of Central Asia where millions are still held in darkness.

The valley of slum communities across the third world where drugs, poverty and hopelessness are rampant.

The valley of Western Europe where the giants of secularism, the occult and atheism reign.

Where do you stand today? On the hill or in the valley?

It is always easier to be with the majority of God's people. It's safer on the mountain. You can stay up there till you die. Or you can make your way down to the battlefield.

The Bible tells us about David, a young shepherd boy. He is too young to be a soldier but he has 3 brothers in the army.

One day his Dad calls him, ***"David, take this basket of roasted grain and these ten loaves of***

bread, and carry them quickly to your brothers." (1 Samuel 17: 17 NLT)

As David arrives, the Philistine and Israelite forces are facing each other. But as soon as the giant appears, the whole army of Israel runs away from him.

When David sees Goliath he turns to the soldiers and says, ***"Who is this pagan Philistine anyway, that he is allowed to defy the armies of the living God?" (1 Samuel 17:27 NLT)***

The majority is too scared to face the giant. The minority (one young man) is ready to stand up for God.

Edmund Burke, a well known philosopher once wrote that "for the triumph of evil, all that is necessary is for good men to do nothing".

Where do you belong?

The day you decide to go onto the battlefield and face the giants, don't expect everyone to get excited.

David's own brothers looked down on him, ***"What are you doing around here anyway?" he demanded "What about those few sheep you're supposed to be taking care of?" (1 Samuel 17: 28 NLT)***

The king himself makes things worse by saying, ***"Don't be ridiculous! There's no way you can fight this Philistine and possibly win! You're only a boy and he's been a man of war since his youth." (1 Samuel 17: 33 NLT)***

If you decide to spend your next summer holidays helping out in a refugee camp, you won't make everybody happy.

If you announce you are off with a mission to fight giants in Niger, Bhutan or Indonesia, your friends won't all be cheering.

The day your family sees you leave the hill of comfort and head for the valley of God's service, they probably won't understand.

Where is the valley God is calling you to?

What are the giants God has called you to face?

There are still not enough workers in the valley. The giants will not fall by themselves.

God is looking for people who will go, regardless of the cost.

In different parts of the world I have met ordinary men and women in all kinds of valleys, slaying giants for Jesus.

I think of Martin and his wife Dari, who for years have been rescuing girls from Cambodia's sex industry.

Or Dave, in the state of Utah in America facing the giant of Mormonism. Hundreds have found Christ through his ministry.

Or Ali, a born again Algerian who passionately reaches out to his fellowmen across the great valley of North Africa.

None of those 3 servants of God know each other. But they have one thing in common: they have responded to the call.

On two occasions I have visited the ministry of Bill Wilson in New York City. When he arrived in the 70s on the 'battlefield of Brooklyn' he faced huge giants: gangs, rape, violence, drugs, prostitution... He started out by himself in ministering to street kids.

Today he has the biggest Sunday school in America. Every week more than 30,000 children are exposed to the Gospel. Bill is over 60 years old now, but has no plan of retiring. He will stay in the valley till the Lord calls him home.

Don't head back to the hill. Every month 1,200 pastors across America quit the ministry. Don't join them.

David then picked up five smooth stones from a stream.

God has given you stones. He has anointed you and He has equipped you. Don't keep your stones in your pockets! Use your sling. He has given you all you need to face the giants.

Amy Carmichael, great missionary to India once said, "We have all eternity to celebrate the victories, but only a few hours before sunset to win them."

Remember: When you walk out onto the battlefield, you are not alone. God is with you.

The same David wrote in the famous 23rd Psalm, ***"Even when I walk through the darkest valley, I will not be afraid, for you are close beside me." (Psalm 23:4 NLT)***

Whether you are slaying giants in a rundown hospital in Mali or in a remote village in Greece, He is with you.

If you're not in a valley, look for one and get busy!

Chapter 9

Have You Seen The Beggar At The Gate?

Peter and John are heading to the 3 o'clock prayer meeting. It must have been something to have those great men of God at the service.

As the two apostles arrive at the Temple, they notice a lame man being carried to the gate of the Temple called "The Beautiful". One thing is sure, this poor man's life was anything but beautiful! For how many years has he been begging at that same spot? 10 years? 20 years?

I live in a country with a lot of beggars. I see them every day.

Today at the Gate of God's Kingdom, there is a beggar.

Just outside the Church, there is a broken world. A world begging for hope, for peace and for a new life. Millions of souls are sitting at the Gate.

Many people that day had probably walked past the beggar as they entered the Temple. Over the years, they have seen him so many times that they did not see him anymore.

Like a nice painting on the wall in your living room. You see it every day but you probably can't describe it accurately if you were asked to!

Millions of children living on the streets... We don't see them anymore.

A multitude of broken lives lying in darkness in the slums, prisons, refugee camps and mental hospitals. We don't see them anymore.

Over one billion Muslims without Jesus, sitting at the Gate... We don't see them anymore.

Most Christians have no interest in North Africa. No interest in the multitudes without Christ in Central Asia. No interest in reading about the Unreached People Groups of the world.

For a lot of Christians, it doesn't matter that 23% of the world has never once heard the Gospel, as long as they get a good seat in the temple!

Some of God's people are so busy going from one Christian conference to another, flipping from one Christian TV channel to another, they've forgotten about the beggar at the Gate.

Some have never even checked outside the temple to see if there could be someone at the Gate!

"I don't have any silver or gold for you," says Peter. ***"But I'll give you what I have. In the Name of Jesus Christ the Nazarene, get up and walk!" (Acts 3:6 NLT)***

You and I have what Peter and John had. Jesus, living in you. We have what money will never be able to give. Only Christ can restore a broken world. Only Christ can bring forgiveness and lasting peace.

The apostles did not just see the lame man. They got involved. ***"Then Peter took the lame man by the right hand and helped him up."*** It's not enough to know the facts. It's not enough to watch every day on the News the great needs of the world. It's not enough to read a newsletter from missionaries overseas. It's not even enough to give to a mission organization. We need to meet the man at the Gate.

Charles Spurgeon, the great English preacher, many years ago, wrote: *"Millions have never heard the name of Jesus. Hundreds of millions know nothing of our King. Shall we let them perish? Can we go to our beds and sleep while China, India, Japan and other nations are being damned? Are we clear of their blood? Have they no claim upon us?"*

I remember reading a book about an American missionary reaching out to the lost in India through an evangelistic film on the life of Jesus.

In the last chapter he shares when he and his family were back in the US once taking meetings, preaching and sharing about the great needs of the people in India. In one church of about two hundred, the missionary's son, John–he was just five years old at the time, was seated about eight rows back on the center aisle. He liked to draw, but on that night he was very attentive as his father spoke to the congregation.

While in the middle of the sermon, without an invitation, the little boy slid off his seat and ran down the aisle, dropped to his knees, his big blue eyes flowing with tears. His body shaking, he cried, *"We've got to do something, Daddy. We've got to help those people!"*

A little 5 year old boy moved by the needs in India. He could see the crippled man, on the other side of the world, begging at the Gate.

"The beggar jumped up, stood on his feet, and began to walk! Then, walking, leaping, and praising God, he went into the Temple with them." (Acts 3: 8 NLT)

What should have been two men walking into the temple, became three!

We don't want to walk into Heaven alone. We want to bring the beggars with us. Our broken world has the right to come into God's Kingdom too. Jesus died for all.

The Gate is open!

Over the years in Cambodia, I have spent a lot of my time helping children stop working on the streets so they can go back to school.

But I have tried to make my priority that each one of those boys and girls has the opportunity to walk through the Gate of the Temple.

I want to stay busy at the Gate.

When the man walked into the temple, the people worshiping ***"realized he was the lame beggar they had seen so often". (Acts 3: 10 NLT)***

So often we've seen the needs. *So often* we've heard about those without Christ. *So often* we've been encouraged to reach the lost.

You probably don't have to hear it again. You probably don't even have to read another missionary book. You don't have to sit under another missionary's talk. All you need to do is to get going.

CPSIA information can be obtained at www.ICGtesting.com
Printed in the USA
BVOW05s0309090115

382499BV00029B/10/P